# The JOURNEY from Love Birds to Loaded Parents



NISHA GAUD

BlueRoseONE.com
Stories Matter

First Published in June 2022

**ISBN: 978-93-5628-593-4**

**eBook ISBN: 978-93-5628-594-1**

**BLUEROSE PUBLISHERS**
www.BlueRoseONE.com
info@bluerosepublishers.com
+91 8882 898 898

**Cover Design:**
Muskan Sachdeva

**Typographic Design:**
Pooja Sharma

**Distributed by:** BlueRose, Amazon, Flipkart

Don't let your emotions cripples your genius, No two generations are same in mind or soul !!!!!

(Nish)

# Introduction

When the author of this book wrote about a small girl who lost her aspirations because of darkness in the world, it was because she had grown up to provide counsel to her own children so they wouldn't make the same mistake she made.

I'm Nisha Gaud the author **of "The Journey from Love Birds to Loaded Parents".**

Do some self-reflection by looking at the heroic men and women who have conquered homelessness, travelled into the wilderness on their own and triumphed against evil individuals. To me, a strong person is able to look at life's challenges as opportunities to learn and grow. To be considered a strong person, one must be self-assured, brave, and truthful. There are certain character qualities that shine out more than others in a strong person, and this strength is derived from the union of life's essentials such as health, spirit, discipline, accountability, and love. It all depends on how you define a person's mental, physical, and emotional strength. In this book, I'll light a candle for you and teach you how to cope with the poison and evil that lurks in the souls of certain individuals. Every hurdle you will encounter throughout your journey, whether you're alone or joined by your soul mate or children can be overcome provided you have the proper tools and resources to cope with it. To turn on the light in a thoughtful manner is all that's required, since the world is going to change and no two generations are same in mind or soul. Life before and after the marriage isn't the same. Parents need to be more resilient and clever in order to help their children succeed. If you had the opportunity, what advice would you give your children? after all your life, you will change after being married and after having children; you will be confronted with a lot of concerns, problems, and questions; nevertheless, you will not know what to do, how to cope with them. Finally, what you say to other people matters, thus you should educate yourself on the reasons behind this fact. Do you want to discover the reason why stress and a messy mom are not a problem after all, considering that we are all humans? Today's parents are under a lot of stress, but do you know why? This is a contentious issue that necessitates a wide range of opinions, but you'll find the ideal answer in this book, one that will show your youngster the right road moving forward.

It's incredibly good to wake up in the morning understanding that God has given me another day to live, Thank you God for the best gift in my life from my Florentine Kids Hridaam and Vani who gave me the power to be strong in writing this book, to my half soul great husband who always was beside me.

Dear parents,

Every child has its own wing to soar. What they all need is just a little push to soar. They don't always require advice, but affection from their parents. Caring it's very important. Don't ever compare them to others since every kid has his own pace. Every youngster has his own capabilities his own ambitions his own aspirations. Show them how to follow their heart, and how to listen to their hearts to accomplish their dreams. Each of us has our own way of living and life after marriage is pretty different from being single , moreover after having kids ,you may experience an issue but don't worry its absolutely natural and any couple goes through it. I composed this book through darkness of a sad girl who had all her dreams fading in front of her eyes and couldn't rebuild her life but only gave it to her children in a shape of advice.

Mrs. Nisha Gaud

# Contents

# Section A

# Story Of Two Love Birds

The union of two persons is referred to as a marriage. Two people join forces to begin a new chapter in their lives. Getting married is a multi-cultural, multi-religious, and multi-community endeavour. There are many different kinds of marriage, such as unions formed out of love or unions arranged.

Their first year together was absolutely the best year that they have passed together, and their love was so exceptional that everyone was envious of them. Love while we are still students isn't always a stable thing that our life will see. This reminds me of a story about a handsome boy named David and a beautiful girl named Rosie who met in college. Their first year together was the best year that they have passed together. They used to kiss one other when they saw each other in the morning, and it was a wonderful display of their love in front of everyone else's eyes whenever they went outside together for lunch after the lesson. It was such a wonderful couple that everyone talked about the party that night when she was clothed with the red robe, and they danced together. After that party, he used to ask her for marriage, and she accepted. Their pure love was incredible, but they didn't know what life was about to show them. Only married adults are privy to this particular truth at this point. They were always known as the couple who cared solely about themselves and never about anyone else or anything else. Even though they spend a lot of time together at the restaurant and parties, the only thing that seems to matter to them is how well they do on their tests. It was the only obligation that they had to fulfil. David and Rosie did not yet realize that marriage is a separate step, which they will learn about in the future. Passionate love is an emotion, whereas marriage is an agreement between two people. It's not always kisses and sex; being married means you must be someone responsible, and there are a lot of things to think about; it's not always a love tale. David and Rosie were overjoyed to learn that they will spend the rest of their lives together. To celebrate this wonderful news, the couple decided to throw a huge party and invite all their close friends. It was a large celebration, and all their parents, members of their families, and friends were present there. After a lengthy dance performance by the pair in front of everyone else at the party, it was eventually over, and everyone headed back to his house. David and Rosie headed to their house to spend their first night together. It was midnight, and their first night together was unique and wonderful for each of them. They each felt the body of the other, and for the first time, they were able to sense that they are for one other. After that night, the days were completely peaceful, and the two of them went on a lot of dates together. They never seemed to be too busy for one another. Until a day when David and Rosie decided to be parents, oh my god, they were laughing when they decided to. They have no idea about having a baby. David was the type of guy who believes that having a child is a simple matter of having one joyful night. Because Rosie is a woman and because she has learned this fact from her mother, she is aware that pregnancy is a challenging experience; however, the idea that becoming parents is a simple process was not something that ever crossed their minds. Rosie discovered that she was pregnant, and the day they found out the wonderful news was a happy and happy day for all of them. The impending arrival of their child prompted David and Rosie to rush out and stock up on new items while also sprucing up their child's bedroom. They are overjoyed and make preparations for a strategy to ensure that their child will receive an excellent education. It is very amusing to watch the couple make plans for their trip while assuming that it is a common route to take. Thinking that the baby will either help them make plans or even give them advice about how to care for him, they were under the impression that the baby would do both. It was the birthday of their son, a lovely one with big eyes, such a huge gorgeous moment for the couple who had spent many years waiting for that moment. Rosie had started to feel strange one night, and David rushed to take her to the hospital. It was the day after their son's birthday. After that day, everyone went to their house bearing gifts, and a lot of elderly men and women shared their wisdom with David and Rosie regarding the impending responsibility that is about to befall them. Rosie and David didn't even bother to give it a second thought. Their way of thinking and their perspective on life leads them to ask, "I mean, it's just a baby, right?" But when they see the truth, they will never get over their surprise again. Because it isn't as simple as just taking care of the baby by itself.

Once you read books you may think that life after marriage is very easy and simple. Loved-up couples can communicate when they marry. They'll dispute everything, big or small. No one makes life decisions without the other. In a dispute, they can find a win-win solution. Children have many arguments, but they can resolve them. Their thinking and decision-making styles won't differ much. They'll help each other conquer hurdles. But in the reality it's very different, you are not going to live with a robot, and you will find yourself handling a lot of responsibilities at the same time. The story of David and Rosie is the best example. They found themselves in such a big dilemma as David always said. He used to call it a dilemma, because of what has been changed in his life. "Where is that romantic guy who used to say always love words and called me angel before," Rosie asked. "Long gone." She replied to her question. It was the moment when they discovered what they are about to live.

They have recently received the exciting news that they will be parents for the first time. They were not equipped to deal with the highs and lows that were to come from the beginning. They questioned their ability to be responsible adults and raise a child. The pleasant event took place, and when they brought the new born infant home, they recognized for the first time that they were parents.

"Who said that our life will be like that, I didn't know the meaning of sleep for five days," David said.

"What about me? Do you want me to start complaining too? "Rosie yelled.

"You are always complaining about everything. It's not the first time." David replied.

"Excuse me this is our child, remember?" Rosie said.

"Stop screaming the doctor said that screaming isn't good for the boy," David said and then he left the room.

"Then he left the room in front of my eyes." Rosie was talking to herself.

Life has changed a lot, they have no more time for each other. Being a mother can be quite humorous at times. It's hilarious in its irony and wit. Motherhood is a lot of different things, but I think the words "funny" and "ironic" do the best job of describing it

"My mother and other women I knew were always caught red-handed engaging in the most embarrassing behaviours in public. I don't know, and I may be exaggerating a little bit, but when I was a very young girl, I committed myself that I would never become THAT woman. You are aware of exactly what I am referring to when I say "the woman who has no idea what she is doing." The one who appears to require a nap has unattractive hair and is carrying two babies at once. Yes, I said it. You need a NAP, lady!" Rosie told her friend who visited to see her situation and her new life.

They went to the store looking for milk for the baby but were unsuccessful in their search. This was the moment when their lives took a complete about-face.

"Why didn't you tell me earlier, when there was still time?" David asked.

I wasn't paying attention, so I missed the fact that there was only one bottle left. In response, Rosie said.

"Oh my god, where on earth are we going to find it if we didn't find it here?" David inquired, prompting him to become agitated.

"What gives, that you didn't notice it? Why am I carrying everything on my back? Because I am a human and because I did not choose to have this child by myself, I need your assistance. You never do anything but sleep, and when you're not doing that, you're probably working. You are now responsible for the upbringing of our child as well. David was forced to apologize in front of an irate woman because Rosie yelled at him, and he had no choice but to admit that it was his fault. That was very clear; never get into an argument with a woman because you will be the one who comes out on the losing end, and she will invariably be right.

They were about to go to sleep, going home after a long day, with their hair dishevelled, their face ugly, and their face sad.

"I'm very tired, I need some sleep," Rosie said.

David inquired, "What about the baby, you need to prepare for him his milk," referring to the infant.

When Rosie confronted him with an angry expression on her face, he realized that it was his responsibility to prepare the meal rather than hers. The infant continued to fuss, indicating that he was extremely hungry; when the sun was finally about to set, the child was given his bottle, and the rest of the family retired to bed for the night.

"Oh no, not again!" David stated. Because the new born has begun to cry and it is currently 2:00 in the morning, one of them will have to get up to make the bottle for the infant because the infant has begun crying. David waited and waited for what seemed like minutes, and eventually, Rosie made the decision to let them do whatever they pleased with complete autonomy. David was very upset about this. As a result, he got out of bed and started preparing himself for himself.

After a year, the baby had grown a little, and they had some experience of how to take care of a baby, so they thought that it would be easy for them to take care of a second child since they had done very well with the first one. This was because they had done very well with the first child.

Are you certain that you want to have a second one? David asked.

"Sure, and why not? Our very first attempt was successful in every way. In response, Rosie said.

"Oh my gosh! Take a good look at yourself; your eyes remind me of the eyes of a panda. David stated.

"Come on, you need to take yourself and this situation a little more seriously, and you need to stop talking about my eyes." Rosie stated.

"Okay, I agree with you, we need to have a second child, let's make for him a brother," you said. "Let's make for him a brother," David answered.

When they talked about having an experience with their first child, they didn't expect a horror movie to play out before their very eyes. Life was just going to laugh at them.

Rosie felt again pregnant; she was happy but also scared. Her mom came once home when Rosie told her about the pregnancy news.

“You are pregnant again? Oh, my darling, why do you have to rush like this?” her mom said.

“Why are you telling me that mom?” Rosie replied.

“Don’t you remember? You asked me once if the baby should drink milk every time he cries.” The mom said.

“Mom! That was my first child I didn’t have much experience.” Rosie said.

“What about David? Does he already know?” the mom asked.

“He is my husband, of course, he already knew.” Rosie said.

“Oh, you don’t need to have a lot of kids now. Remember you are still young and David too, and make sure to have some time for you and your first child first. Now you are pregnant make sure that everything goes very well.” her mom said.

“Do you know mom when I look to my single friend, and when I compare her life to mine, for example, I sometimes find myself wishing I hadn't been a mother. Other times, I'm glad I did it. Because of this, I have a distinct impression that I am a very low-class individual.” Rosie said.

“It’s okay my darling, you are such a great mother, don’t worry everything will pass.” Her mom said.

When you can't take care of things anymore and have no other option but to fight back, it will be too late to stop having children. Parents who have already had their first child will want to have another child after they have had their first child.

The arrival of the second child signals the start of the terrifying movie; what the heck is going on? The ideal couple: the stunning woman, who used to be concerned about her appearance, is now only concerned about the baby bottle, and the doting boyfriend, who used to ask for new flowers for his girlfriend, is about to look up the size of a baby diaper.

“He sleeps only when we are awakened, did you notice that?” David asked.

“Oh I want some sleep, my head wants to explode,” Rosie said.

“Oh my god who said that we are going to experience all of that, I think our first one didn’t do what this one did,” David said and he was looking at his child with weird eyes. Rosie laughed and said,” do you remember this one is your child too.”

Naturally, in the past, young families focused all of their spare time on spending quality time together, relaxing, and having fun. Some went to work or school. The children's parents have the luxury of letting their parents do anything they want with their free time. Having a child, on the other hand, brings about significant life adjustments. Therefore, a child demands a significant amount of one's time and energy. You are correct; it consumes all of your time and leaves you with no forces.

Rosie and David went through the second experience together, and this time, not only Rosie but also David had the eyes of a panda. Because he was unable to get very much sleep, he would sometimes  sleeping while at work, even though his boss would always argue with him. After all, David is a new parent who does not have a lot of experience, and Rosie tried to call her mother to get some assistance. All of David's friends are aware that he is having trouble sleeping; after all, he is a new parent.

“I told you before that you shouldn’t have more kids until the first one grows a little” her mom said.

“I’m tired mom!” Rosie said.

Crying can be heard coming from every room in the house; their first child can be found in every crevice, refusing to let anything take its place; and their second child is perpetually hungry and wants his mother to be with him. The couple's life was made significantly more challenging by the experience of taking care of their two infant children at the same time. They no longer have the time to spend with one another because all that matters to them now is the baby drinking milk from a bottle, changing diapers, and sleeping. They need to eat quickly to care for the baby, and Rosie does not have time to waste. Rosie, who used to make only delicious dishes for David to eat, is now making fast food. But it's not just any fast food; it's bread with cheese.  David came home from work, he hugged his children and his wife, and then he fell asleep in the living room. The house is a complete disaster right now;

nothing is in the spot where it was originally kept. In the end, after two years, their life becomes more stable; the two children mature; the couple has adjusted to the situation, and some peace has returned to the house; everything was going well until they were invited to a wedding of a mutual friend. At that point, they went to the home of some friends when they received the invitation. It wasn't like it used to be there were now four of them, and the bride and groom were not allowed to bring their children to the ceremony. David and Rosie were at a loss as to what to do, how to deal with the situation, and where they should leave their children.

"I believe that we ought to allow them to stay at your parent's house," David said.

"That will drive my mother insane, and she will never put up with these two demons," I said. In response, Rosie said.

"We don't have a choice; we have to go get some rest right now," said the speaker. David said.

When they arrived at Rosie's house, her mother yelled at them, "I'm not the one who decided to be pregnant twice as you know, you two!"

"Please, mom, it's only for one night, it's the wedding of our best friend, and we have to be there," the children pleaded with their mothers. Rosie said.

They went to the party, which didn't take too much time, and when they came back, the surprise was already set up and waiting for them. Thankfully, her mother agreed, and they let the children stay there while they went to the party. As soon as they opened the door, they saw Rosie's mother running into the house ahead of the children with her hair flying all over the place. She is screaming, "Come take your monsters from me!" as she does so. David and Rosie were quick to gather the kids and head back to their own homes after dropping them off.

"I informed them that my mother is unable to look after them," Rosie remarked, and she is fully aware that this will be the final occasion on which her mother agrees to watch her younger siblings.

Life was peaceful, but it was that routine that every couple will go through at some point. That is until Rosie started feeling pregnant, even though neither she nor David had planned for it. Here the hell opened its door for the couple, now they have three children, let's describe the scene, Rosie and David are in the living room looking at their three kids, the first one is fighting with the second one, and the third one crying for milk. David and Rosie just looking sadly at their situation that hasn't any other solution but to accept it, after this is the life after kids and every couple must pass through it, this is necessary.

Rosie's attention gradually shifts away from her husband, David, and toward herself and the baby as she prepares to become a mother. Naturally, this results in a shift in their sexual relations.

I am aware that I do not stand alone. However, it is still considered somewhat taboo to acknowledge that parenting can be challenging or that there are aspects of it that we dislike. There is an absurd amount of pressure on parents to provide their children with everything they could want, to celebrate even the most insignificant of their children's accomplishments and to ensure that everything is consistently amazing. Despite this, we are unable to have a conversation that is open and honest about what it is like to live under such pressure and make such sacrifices. When we do complain, we do so in the manner that is considered to be the most socially acceptable, such as by sharing memes that proclaim "the struggle is real" or by discussing how much wine we need to get us through this. We're joking around, but it doesn't feel that funny. It seems as though parts of me, mostly the enjoyable parts, are withering away due to a lack of attention.

Rosie and David had a beautiful life after all because having children is the most gorgeous and enormous gift that God may give to us. Everything passed quickly even they forgot about all that they experienced. The kids have grown up and their parents learned a lot from them. Yes, it's true, children teach parents a lot, how to be patient and wise. The most important is to make sure that life must be full of love. Parents need to maintain control over their children, but they should not behave in a manner that causes their children to fear. Even teachers should not behave in a manner that causes fear in their pupils. Parents need to encourage their children to study and to have self-discipline. If they continue to annoy the children, the children may grow to dislike them. Because they are not very mature, it is important to handle them with tact at all times. When interacting with their offspring, parents should always do so out of a place of love and compassion for their kids. So that they will take from their parents' wisdom and love necessary to be strong in their life.

David and Rosie are examples of true love after such an experience they have kept attached and made an effort to surpass all the obstacles. From little birds to loaded parents, a beautiful couple who met in the college kept their love sacred in their hearts until the day they get married and had kids to share their love with and they lived happily ever after. The gift that God gave to them; they and we must appreciate it always and every day, and we should never forget that there are in this world some people who wish to have such a gift too, but they didn't have that chance.

Everyone who longs to start a family almost always harbours the dream of one day having a contented partnership that is predicated on love. This love, in turn, gives rise to optimism and a fondness for each other that can make many people green with envy. As a result, love is an essential component of every human being and one that calls for a significant amount of dedication and focus. However, for any relationship to be successful, it takes more than simply having feelings of closeness and promising to live together with one another while maintaining a commitment to the ideals of a relationship for both parties. It is also important to keep in mind that it takes work and time to develop the kind of loving, trusting, and positive connection that is characteristic of a relationship characterized by love. When one or both partners can distinguish between the facts and their feelings, they can view the other more objectively and not through the lens of any perceived shortcomings in the relationship that they may have.

# Section B

## Part-1

# Girls Not Bride

*"Make yourself in such a way that you are always a part of solution , not the problem"*

When it comes to our births, we have very little influence over the course of our lives. Our lives take on more meaning and purpose as we get older. It is essential that you take your life's objective into account. Keep vigilance, eliminate weakness, and become stronger than ever in your life. Learn to express yourself authentically from the inside out, regardless matter whether you are timid and soft-spoken or loud and outspoken. When you are surrounded by so many signals that tell you what you should think, feel, and do, it is practically hard to remain objective, so try always to be your own hero.

Even though you've heard stories of societies that see girls as incomplete and hence exterminate them, I can assure you that these stories are not made up. In fact, they are very much alive and well. Many people throughout the world still believe that women should stay at home and not talk or think aloud. Marriages are predetermined for certain members of particular families. Someone else, maybe a member of the couple's family, is the one who puts the two of them together. Each individual is free to decide for themselves whether or not they wish to proceed with the marriage, and their families are obligated to respect any decision they make in this regard.

It's a story of a child, Rosey lived in a poverty-stricken household with her father and elder brother, and even her mother was swayed by their shameful gazes. Her mother had hoped for a boy rather than a daughter. Rosey's life was filled with limitations; she was unable to fiRosie her schooling and was relegated to doing only household work. They all stopped her whenever she tried to do anything, saying "you would bring shame to the house". She had no idea what it meant to love or to choose the guy she would spend the rest of her life with.

Her teen's time was very complicated with problems and sadness, she used to see some families who let their girls studying, learning, independent, the time she used to work as a maid in her house. It was difficult to her to accept that life because humans were born free from their mothers, who dares to make a human being inside a cage only because of society and its mistaken ideas about women. Every person has a unique experience of what it means to become a parent. The reality of being a new parent covers a wide range of different feelings: love, fear, exhilaration, exhaustion, confusion, and chaos, to name just a few, and Rosey before becoming an adult and a mother had a sad experience that made her stronger than ever.

It all happened so quickly that she ended herself in a forced marriage to a man she didn't love or choose, but her father did. He believes that he has chosen her spouse and that he is the family's wisest member and knows what's best for her. A person by the name of David had pushed her to be married to him. She can't obtain a divorce since it's against the law, and if she did, her father wouldn't let her back into the house. With her husband's family, she must be accommodating. Her legs were hurting her every day but she couldn't tell anyone. She was wondering if her husband will divorce her because of that. She couldn't refuse to see his family member ever week and prepare for them dinner, they came without any invitation without asking her. It's David's house and not hers, she is only a maid who will serve David and take care of his children.

When Rosey became pregnant for the first time in a long time, she was shocked by the reaction of her husband, his parents, and everyone else she knew. Parents like Rosey's were eager for a boy child. She gave birth to a daughter after nine months of illness and pain. A shameful look spread over their faces the second time the doctor told them of the news. An unhappy spouse is a bad sign for the family and must be dealt as such. Her existence was made a misery by the arrival of gloom and doom in the house. She has never been treated as she desired. She had such an experience from her father's home, but now sadness captured her soul and made her feeling guiltier of having a daughter. It's the same sentiment that her mother had. Some type of horrible feeling that will be inherited from a generation to another one. This type of traditions of putting the woman in a bad condition and no authority to have for choosing her life or anything concern her is something injured a lot of girls spirits and stole their dreams and objectives from them, and It's unfair to lower down their power. Life must give everyone happiness a boy or a girl. Every spirit in this world must reach what it wants.

Our entire lives are spent anticipating the possibility that something terrible will happen, something that will rob us of everything we've worked for and lead us to the stage of love disappointment that nearly every serious intimate relationship, and probably every one that lasts longer than a day, has to deal with.

After her wedding to David, Rosey had a very difficult time adjusting to her new life and making peace with it. Her life was on the verge of being taken by misery. She worked as the housemaid, and before to that, she had also done cleaning work for his family. She was only there to serve the guy and his family, thus she was unable to voice her opinion on anything since the man is the only one who makes decisions inside the family. She was only there to serve the man. Rosey, who was at the beginning of the story, had come to terms with the fact that it was too late to alter anything. A person's marriage is the beginning of a new chapter in their life, but Rosey's spirit had been destroyed by the fire. She had worked from sunrise to night, and all she could think about was what to make for dinner. On top of that, she was responsible for taking care of his elderly parents, both of whom had personalities that might be described as demanding and strict. David was the stereotypical kind of conservative guy who was never concerned with how she was feeling. He is only concerned with his children and the object of his desire. Rosey discovered she was pregnant once again with twins, this time with a girl and a boy. The family finally experienced joy, but it wasn't enough to erase the pain she had been through all these years before it. She was unable of forgetting what they had said about her or the way in which they had treated her. Perhaps she will behave as if she forgot, even though the fact is that she did not forget. Actually, she will never forget the days that she was wed against her will to a guy she never loved since that was the day that her dreams died. She will always remember that. At least there's something we can't force ourselves to do: something you can fake a grin or convey but not the truth in your heart, like love for your spouse. It will never fail to inform you of your identity. Integrity and sincerity reside deep inside your soul.

Rosey had been abused by her husband in front of their children for many occasions, even in front of his parents who didn't even utter a thing to stop. No one did care about her bodily or emotional wellbeing. All what they stated is that she had to be patient, and this the marriage, and what she was meant to see or obtain. She is here just to serve him, and take care of his kids. When she felt unwell they was gazing at her with the looks of pity and that she is too weak, they didn't care to help her. It was the force of god and the prayers that rescued her spirit.

How may a girl be seen as a mistake by others? It's an outright injustice. It's a gift from God to parents, and they should be grateful and say a daily prayer of thanks to him for it, but that's not what happens. People these days have such filthy hearts.

Rosey's life changed radically after she had three children; she had been sad for a long time before her children gave her pleasure. She had given up her dreams and aims, but she could now see the light at the end of the tunnel because she had turned on the light. Throughout the years, Rosey recognized that she couldn't allow her children to make the same mistake she had done. For the sake of her children, she took the choice to be a strong woman. To be clever, one must comprehend that Rosey is the builder of a new generation that must grasp the truth of the world around them and realize that females are more than a slave or a mistake. A mother's counsel on how to enjoy a healthy life free of mental and physical ailment was the finest gift she could offer her children. She was particularly worried about the boy's behaviour toward his younger sister. She strained every ounce of her energy to convince him to discard his preconceived views. To be a strong, independent woman who isn't afraid to say no or voice her opinion, especially when it comes to selecting who she will spend the rest of her life with, is something that her mother instilled in her.

Rosey never stopped being happy and loving toward her children, and she ever saw her daughter as anything other than a powerful and competent young lady. Rosey's children were her greatest source of pride and love. She used to let her brother and her argue about everything and figure out a solution together so that her brother would be persuaded and realize that there is no difference in the mind of a boy or a girl and that everyone has the capacity to think and determine what is best for themselves. She wanted him to realize that there is no difference in the mind of a boy or a girl and that everyone has the capacity to think and determine what is best for them.

The loss of her objectives left her with little alternative but to let the past, her sorrowful memories, and the rising of life pass her by. Instead, she chose to get back up and teach her children how to grow in a normal manner in order to combat the darkest spirits in this terrible world, who will not feel pity for a sad, depressed girl for a single second. Screaming will not be heard, but the strength and might of the demonstrators will be.

"In time, you'll begin to worry about the future of our world. Our children's futures will be formed by what the world becomes, and we want to give the greatest possible environment for them to grow up in." Rosey had something to say about it.

As a poor girl who was extremely weak, she became quite powerful and had children to teach them how to improve the world and make it a better place to live in. Her books and quotations will serve as a way for her to leave her mark on this gloomy world, and she will do the same for her children so that they might do the same for their own children in the future, from a generation to another until the society would remove the old murderous traditions, and replaced with honesty, love, prayers, peace, purpose, and especially spirit caring, It is the complete core of your pleasure and where your heart's wishes dwells.

Hye mommy try this whenever you feel exhausted:

1. Put on Comfortable clothing
2. Manage your time and divide your house chores hours in small blocks
3. Get healthy snacks and plenty of water in between
4. Organise your things well to get it on time and though unnecessary or broken stuff right away
5. Turn off all distraction while taking rest
6. Take a break and have a fun sometimes

# Part- 2

# Journey of Motherhood

*"A mother carries herself in all circumstances, but when it comes to her child, she is not afraid to go against the entire world!!!"*

# Mom For the First Time.

It was my very first-time experiencing parenthood as a caregiver. My family and my partner went out of their way to shower me with gifts and kind gestures.

Despite the fact that I am not very knowledgeable in this area, I continue to struggle with a variety of health problems and other vexing issues.

The minute I became a mother to my first kid, the trajectory of my life shifted 180 degrees centigrade. My recollection of the agony and sorrow had almost completely disappeared.

As a consequence of the fact that this was my very first time, I made several mistakes. This is why I'm writing it down, so I won't forget it. It's conceivable that you just gave birth, so if that's the case, try not to repeat the same error.

When I went on a date, I made the mistake of attempting to ensure that everyone had a good time, which ultimately resulted in my own unhappiness. I was unable of taking care of myself.

I was unable to tell that the baby was famished and begging for something to eat by the way that it was acting. Because I was under the impression that a baby only must be fed once every two hours, I was unable to stick to this routine.

It's an issue when you feel terrible about your bad habits but don't have a regular routine in place to help you change them. You just need shirts and pyjamas at this point.

Even though I wasn't getting enough sleep and that I was unable to complete the assignment on my own, I didn't seek for aid from anybody.

I have my doubts about whether or not I'll be able to handle it. I'll be able to handle everything on my own due to the help of my child and the kindness of complete strangers who are prepared to provide advice for free. I'll be able to do it all by myself.

Because of the birth of my first child, I committed all these mistakes while I was still young enough to take advantage of opportunities to have fun.

Just know that you are doing a great job as a mother, no matter how rough the days or nights get. You'll be prepared if things go difficult. This is what you were meant to do, and you're doing an incredible job at it, so always be proud of yourself and trust your capacities.

It is common knowledge that there is no manual included with the job of parenting. Although you get support from other women who can relate to what you are going through and can empathize with you, this is not the same thing. For all of the new mothers and moms-to-be out there, it is important to realize that you do not need to figure out everything on your own. It is not inappropriate to seek for help.

# Mom For the Second Time.

I have already promised myself that I won't repeat the errors that I've made in the past. Making errors is a vital part of life. We learn from our errors. Mistakes are the finest lessons of our lives. They are anything that occurs inadvertently and without the awareness of a human being. The only way errors can be prevented is to never do anything. I will be strong, and I will ask for help when I need to because life must be fear. If my children should grow in a safe life I have to make it for them.

My objective is to bring up my baby in the manner that I think to be finest. I desire to make their life devoid from anxiety, challenges, and sicknesses. It's a road that all the parents desire their children to walk in this world. The history that I encountered was a vital lesson to me, thus I will not place my children again in the same scenario.

Do not be hesitant to seek assistance if you feel that you need it. Etiquette will not be asked of anybody during this festivity. However, some of us find it uncomfortable to ask for aid when we need it. Unfortunately, this typically results in unsatisfactory employment and relationships but also in a variety of problems such as burnout or depression. I wonder how the statistics for various diseases and even for suicide rates would look like if we would simply ask for aid when we need it

When the infant is napping, it's time for you to retire in as well. You also need some rest to continue and to have a normal balanced life you have to be strong with a good health situation, otherwise it will offer a terrible effect on your health and your kids, and you will be no longer competent to take care of them. It is not a characteristic to be embarrassed of if one has a neat and well-organized home, so be flexible with your kids so they will feel your love.

My body is in terrific shape owing to the combination of a balanced diet and frequent exercise. So, you must be a healthy food lover, trust me your body will thank you later for it. Furthermore, healthful food is also amazingly delicious as counter to traditional belief. Nowadays, kids need to eat healthy meals more than ever. You must encourage correct dietary habits so that your kids will be healthy and fit.

To contribute something to other people without expecting anything in return, this is the best gift you can have in this life when you feel that your heart is so wide for forgiveness, love and aid, it's the purpose that God had formed us for. Helping each other without expecting any advanced things, that's why I tried to be the pleasant person always, it's a way of life and of course it's not a weakness, but a feature of stronger people.

**Sigma Rule to follow after delivery:**

1. Take your multi vitamins and iron supplements on time
2. Fall in love with the healthy
3. Learn to deal with stress
4. Practice more time with sunshine
5. Allow yourself to be happy
6. Start exercising regularly
7. Practice gratitude
8. See everything you experience as a gift from God
9. Express your feelings
10. Drink a nutritious smoothie

## Baby Sitting or Career.

I can appreciate your viewpoint and anticipate how you will respond to the content of this discussion since I am also a mother. I'm not going to lecture or pass judgment on any of you; rather, I'm simply going to share my thoughts, which are only my own perspective.

In my opinion, the most difficult decision that a woman may face in her life after becoming a mother is deciding whether to choose a profession over providing babysitting services. Many of you will decide on your profession because you believe it to be of utmost significance in this life and because it is through it that you will be able to preserve and provide for your offspring. I am sure that your work will keep you and your children safe, but you must be aware that time will never come around again. You should try to appreciate that moment since it will bring you more love in this life. Even if we do all in our power to ignore the fact, our children are maturing at a startling pace each and every single second of each and every single day. After they have all achieved maturity, this will be the end of the story. That chunk of time is lost forever. There is no way to get it back. Being a parent who remains at home with their children around the clock may be challenging at times, but you'll never be able to turn back the hands of time or make them as young as they were when you first had them. You also won't be able to make them as old as you were when you first had them. Financial concerns play a significant role in the decision-making process for some families over which parent will stay at home and take care of the children as well as the household duties. The expense of providing day-care may soon pile up. It's likely that almost all the money you make each week goes toward paying for your childcare costs if you have small children and pay for day-care or a nanny. When you are determining how much your salary is in comparison to the cost of day-care, be sure to consider all the additional expenses that are associated with childcare, such as the cost of gas and the clothes you wear to work, in addition to the amount of time and effort that is required to transport your child to and from day-care. Additionally, the costs of childcare may vary quite a bit from one region to another. As a result, if the rates in your area are higher, it is more likely that you will not be able to earn a living by working outside the home.

It's up to you to choose.

**Mommy Make time for yourself :**

1. Practice self love and acceptance
2. Wake up 15 minutes earlier in the morning
3. Wake up with gratitude
4. Read something new everyday
5. Try to make your own happiness
6. Visit your loved once very often
7. Fill you home with real happiness, positivity and greenery
8. Be ok with your own process
9. Focus on your physical fitness
10. Pamper your self at least once in a week
11. Smile without a reason

## Your words matter

Do Words Matter? Words have an incredible amount of power, and there are instances when the words we use might offend other people. The freedom to express oneself is greatly valued; but, what should be done when someone else's enjoyment of that freedom causes them discomfort or insults them? There is such a wide variety of different types of people, and each one is irritated by a unique set of circumstances. In this day and age, when we are freer to say whatever is on our minds, we are witnessing an increasing trend of people taking offence at the things that are being uttered. It might be difficult to see how some phrases can be construed as insulting to a person, especially when you might not see it that way.

Throughout human history, people have consistently discovered new and inventive ways to look down on unique individuals. They accomplish this goal by coming up with phrases that openly insult a person based on the particular qualities that make up that individual.

The inquiry "how can I help you?" is an effective way to reassure someone agitated or frantic that he or she is important and that someone is willing to assist and listen to their concerns instead of simply saying "calm down."

Tears, you idiotic tears! Always showing up at the most inopportune times. Now that everyone on the street is gazing at you, your eyes are starting to blur, and as a result, you trip over the bumper and fall into the street. What a klutz. How embarrassing! Why do you feel the need to weep like this all the time? Crying isn't a sign of weakness but a sign of courage, so stop crying I can see this is hard for you, but you have to be strong so you can stand always and fight in this life.

When someone else is going through a challenging time, we tend to underestimate the importance of just listening to them talk about it. You are alright, in response to another query asking the same thing, and having both a different tone and a distinct meaning.

You have control over the words you use, but you do not have control over the effect those words have on other people. Because of this, it is vital to keep a low level of speaking at all times. It's strange how some individuals may assume that they are asking very ordinary and common questions, but the very precise questions that they ask may be a little frustrating to others because they just point out the obvious, or they may even be insulting occasionally. It's amusing how some individuals may assume that they are asking quite regular and common inquiries. Stop yelling take a deep breath and tell me what happens

Probably, feeling melancholy is not one of your top preferences, but it's crucial to keep in mind that the emotion does exist, and it's quite normal to experience it sometimes. Allowing yourself to experience sadness, even though it may be unpleasant, may have several beneficial benefits in your life.

It's quite typical for people to avoid feeling sad because they believe it's a "bad" emotion and label it as such. You may find yourself turning to diversions, such as scrolling through your phone or nibbling even if you're not hungry, to stave off the heavy sensation that's developing in your chest.

When someone brings up a subject that is painful for you, attempting to avoid feeling sad may sometimes manifest itself as an aggressive response.

Trying to steer clear of negative emotions may also come with a dose of poisonous optimism. Toxic positivity is the practice of ignoring negative feelings in favour of more positive ones, such as happiness. Toxic optimism might give the impression of being helpful, but it can end up robbing you of your authenticity and taking an emotional toll.

That's enough for you, no more stress, do u need a hug? Let me tell you that a hug gives happiness. Hugs aren't merely nice greetings or a method of being physically connected with someone. It's more than the biological relationship as it also provides health advantages. Hugging you before an event that is likely to be stressful, such as giving a speech or going on a job interview, may be able to help you relax and feel less anxious about the event. When someone hugs you, you can maintain your composure and not lose your composure at any point throughout the embrace. When someone needs to be calmed, people often embrace them for this purpose.

I am over this too I am here for you, While there's nothing wrong with this remark, particularly if it's uttered with passion, you may want to find a better approach to communicate this feeling.

The social values that these words express to both interlocutors and society as a whole are of the highest significance. The semantic meanings of these words are not what are of the utmost importance; rather, it is the social values that they transmit. It is possible that having an awareness of values might successfully assist in the creation of harmonious relationships between persons, in contrast to the fact that possessing semantic knowledge only sets a cap on one's cognitive ability.

Be careful with the words that you choose to speak because one day you will wake up and realize that you have created something; one day someone will come up to you and tell you that your words have changed them; and on that day, you will desire that he would say the most appropriate thing possible.

# Part -3

## Respect personal space.

*" Over protective parents excessively is a curse for the future of children and is always fatal to their mental and physical strength".*

## Be A Good Example For Your Kids.

You can't just bring your children into the world and then walk away from them. Your kids will not learn everything from life and by their own experience, but they will need your help. A respectable youngster must keep such lesson in mind and never conduct the behaviours in the life which make their parent disrespectful in the society.

Most of what kids learn about social graces comes from witnessing their parents. The more you influence them when they are younger, the more they will take your teachings to heart. In the heat of the moment, ask yourself this question: Is this how you want your child to respond when they are angry? Keep in mind that your children are continually keeping an eye on you. According to studies, most children who hit have a parent or guardian who behaves violently.

Respect, kindness, honesty, compassion, and tolerance are some of the values you want your children to demonstrate. Be unselfish in your activities. Do excellent things for the sake of others without seeking recompense. Gratitude and compliments should be expressed. Above all, teach your children respect by treating them the way you want others to treat you.

As you do wonderful actions in front of your children, they'll notice and even emulate your habits. You smile at neighbours, send your mates heart-emoji-filled texts, and cheer on your colleagues. But how many of those nice acts do your kids see? The more good acts you do in front of your children, the more they'll notice and start to duplicate those identical gestures. If you actually want to do right by your children and raise intelligent, honest and loving persons, show them by example. Avoid emotional reactions, reacting in rage may ruin relationships and put you into trouble with authorities. Show your youngsters how to manage their own emotions by reacting calmly to challenging events. If you find yourself wanting to reply in fury, step away until you can get your emotions under control. Explain your selections, there's strength in observing a successful decision, but the biggest lessons may not be evident to a kid. Timeouts or redirections are fantastic examples of times you may justify your behaviour. If you give a youngster a timeout, always explain why. Talk about what your youngster did to violate the rules and how they need time to calm down and think about better ways to manage difficulties. "Because I said so" may work, but it accomplishes nothing for creating a positive example. On the flip hand, talking things out lets your youngster realize that you respect him or her enough to be honest with them. Embrace your shortcomings; no one is an island. Admit your faults when you act in a way that is at variance with how you want your children to behave. If you chance to interrupt someone while they're talking, kindly say apologize and allow them to continue their idea. Keep in mind that your children are humans, too. Do onto others what you would have them do towards you.

When a youngster views herself through the eyes of their parents, they begin to build a sense of self. It's crucial to remember that your kids catch up on everything you say and do. More than anything else, your words and acts as a parent create their sense of self-worth.

Praise for even the slightest victories may increase children's self-esteem, and enabling them to do things on their own can help them build a strong feeling of independence. Belittling comments or unflattering comparisons between youngsters, on the other hand, will make children feel worthless.

It's better not to say or write anything that may be taken out of context or used as a weapon. "What a bad idea!" and "You're behaving more like a baby than your tiny brother!" are just as detrimental to someone's mental health as a physical assault is.

Compassionate communication involves smart word choice. Even if you don't like your children's behaviour, let them know that everyone makes mistakes and you still love them.

Every day, seek for something to be thankful for. Be generous with your praise - your compassion, hugs, and words of encouragement can go a long way and are usually more than enough of a reward in and of themselves. You'll quickly discover that you're "growing" more of the desired behaviour.

One warning, followed by ramifications such as a "time out" or a loss of privileges, may be suitable. When parents don't follow through with sanctions, it's a classic misstep. A parent can't penalize a youngster for speaking up one day and then not puRosie him or her the next. Consistent conduct shows people what to anticipate from you.

Parents and children usually find it difficult to sit down together for a meal, let alone spend time together. Again then, there's probably nothing that children would rather have. If you want to eat breakfast together with your youngster or go for a walk after dinner, wake up 10 minutes earlier in the morning. When their parents aren't paying attention to them, youngsters may misbehave or act out in try to gain their attention.

Make it clear what you expect. In the case of a problem, address it, offer your opinions, and push your youngster to participate with you on a solution. Include the ramifications. Propose fresh ideas and present choices. Be sensitive to your child's suggestions, too. Negotiate.

*" Children who have a role in selecting choices are more likely to follow through on those decisions."*

In order to offer your kid an exceptional education, all you need to do is to instil in them a feeling of self-control and unconditional love. Life is full of unexpected twists and turns, and our children need to be prepared for them, so they will battle and persevere in front of issues and learn how to manage their unpleasant conditions are a responsibility in this life to pass through it. Because of this, listening to them and having a conversation with them is the greatest approach to show them.

**Do this:**

1. Listen to your children
2. Say sorry when you are wrong
3. Say thank you when they do something for you
4. Do not overreact
5. Do not demand your child to be respectful just because you are the parent, True respect can only be earned not demanded
6. Teach them to say "Hello" when you meet someone
7. Respect your child's privacy
8. Once in a day have a meaningful eye to eye conversation with your child

## Difference Is Natural

Life is wonderful and its beauty conceal in the variety we observe every day. The colours are the finest evidence of it. Every hue had his influence on our soul. For that attempting to be like everyone would damage this beauty and create life with no sense. So don't anticipate discovering only one manner or only one colour, since it will never exist the more you embrace diversity in this world the more you will find yourself happy and complete.

Take caution. Sometimes we speak before we've had a chance to consider. The most natural thing in the world to say to our child when we are trying to urge them to do something is something along the lines of, "Why can't you be more like your brother?"

Please don't secretly label your child and make others feel uncomfortable by doing so, moms. The first one I made was a disaster, but the second one turned out fantastic. No matter how many children you have, you should always encourage your kids to be themselves and express themselves freely. The objective of ensuring that the needs of each of your children are met in a manner that is fair and balanced is a vital one. Mom, you need to keep an eye out and make sure your child isn't comparing themselves to other kids.

Every child is one of a kind and has their very own distinct personality, and a different way of thinking, so don't force him to change because he can't and then the consequences will affect his evolution.

Therefore, please refrain from addressing your child in a condescending tone and be soft with them. "Just look at your sister, who is constantly listening, when you don't want to pay attention to what's being spoken" it's a kind of an example that a lot of kids listen to it every day. They will feel like they don't have any confidence and no value. They will even compare himself to everyone not only brothers and sisters. It's mistake that a lot of parents do when they try to convince their kids or show them something. It will also give some kind of hate and darkness in their soul toward their brothers and sisters. They will envy how you use them as an example, and then they will forget their way of progress and evolution in this life. So always remember every child had his own and special way in this life it's natural in this life and you as a parent must notice this, you mustn't change it but accompany it until they reach their purpose in this life. Make sure your children are kind and appreciative with all the folks in their regular lives, such as a bus driver or a waitress, and encourage children to care for those who are vulnerable.

**Say this frequently to your children:**

1. I am so proud of you
2. You are such a great kid
3. You will always be my hero
4. You always make me smile
5. You are such a quick learner
6. Its ok to make a mistake
7. Every problem has solution
8. You are the powerful soul
9. Doesn't matter what we are always with you

## Teach Them Something New

You are both their First and Only Sources of Educational Guidance.

A mother on her voyage of bringing up the kid makes numerous sacrifices on the route, and it is at those times a youngster learns to grow up to be intellectual, loving and sensitive towards other human beings

The main caretakers, educators, and role models for their children are frequently the moms who stay at home.

You are the major impact on children before they join school, and they are relying on you to always teach them something new.

Even if you have a career outside the house, you will still be able to find time to spend with your kids, but the benefits of having a job outside the home greatly outweigh the downsides. In addition, you are the major model that kids look up to and replicate on a daily basis.

It is crucial for parents to develop positive habits in their children as early as possible. This involves encouraging their children to put their toys away and teaching them essential life skills such as how to cook, clean, do laundry, arrange doctor's appointments, read excellent literature, and react correctly to phone calls, among other things.

Inspire your kids by letting them select a charity. For example, before your kids and I remove toys and books, we chose a charity where our contributions will go. It makes it genuine when you know who will get your thing.

Show them compassion. Children also tend not to be able to see the wider picture. Because young children normally concentrate on what's immediately in front of them and tend to not think too far ahead, they may not grasp the full implications of what acts like meanness, exclusion, or bullying may have on other kids. Kids are typically self-centred, which means that they aren't always able to put themselves in the shoes of another person or make an effort to think about how someone else may be feeling. This is because kids are naturally unable to empathize with others. On the other hand, this does not imply that children are by nature cruel.

Your children will become increasingly aware of how much of an impact all of this has on their ability to function well in the world as they become older. However, it is never too early to start teaching children the fundamentals of life, such as how to brush their teeth, how to dial 911 in an emergency, and how to make an appointment with their doctor.

It's also a good idea to get kids into the habit of being friendly and finding something nice to say to someone, and to teach them that don't forget to be a nice kindness teacher. Being rough will not make them learn but only fear of you. It's not what you want to let as a feeling inside your kids heart and soul. Be a kind and kind instructor rather than a strict one.

**Teach your child:**

1. Teach your child to be kind and respectful
2. Teach them basic table manners like wash your hand before eating, chew your food with your closed mouth, say "please the pass " instead of reaching over someone , don't start eating until everyone else does.

3. Teach them conversation manners like look in peoples eye , say " excuse me" to get attention, use kind words , wait for your turn.
4. Don't make bad comment about anyone
5. Don't make rude notices when you step out somewhere.

# Part- 4

# Me And My Little One

The most valuable thing you can give to your child is " quality time"

## Organize A Special Outing For You And Your Youngster.

It is of the utmost importance to spend quality time with one's children. The years will pass quickly, and before you know it, you'll be bidding farewell to children who were only new-borns just a few short years ago. Having said that, investing a significant amount of time in one's offspring is not just required for sentimental or simple "hanging out" purposes with one's offspring. As a parent, you should see the time you spend with your child not only as a chance to form a closer relationship with them but also as a window of time in which you may impart important lessons about life. Quality, not number, should be your first concern.

It is not enough to just stop your child from playing video games; you must also become involved in the process of how they play these games. In point of fact, the market is rife with apps that are both beneficial and educational. In addition to that, you shouldn't just let your kid go out and play by themselves. Allow kids to play their preferred video games while simultaneously encouraging them to demonstrate interest in the real world. It will help you develop a stronger bond with the child and provide you with a better understanding of the appeal of video games like the one you are now playing. It goes without saying that you don't want gaming to consume all of your time, but you also shouldn't completely disregard it as an activity.

A date with your kid implies spending quality time together, which will improve your bond with the youngster.. Take your child for a stroll in the park on a sunny day so that you can listen to what he has to say and show him how much you care about his unique perspective on life. This will boost his self-esteem and make him a better person.

You and your kid will both benefit from an ice cream date at the beach. The spiritual and yoga programs you take will help you and your kid develop a strong relationship with God and a firm belief in the power of fate.

When possible, make and enjoy meals together with your children. Choose meals that are simple and require minimal preparation, or just take an apple and sit down for a few minutes with your kid to talk.

You may demonstrate your love to your child without any particular circumstances by giving him a tight embrace and he will be able to know how much you love and care about him.

It's also a good idea to plan a mini-trip each week, maybe on the weekend, so you can accomplish all of the things I mentioned above. It will also be a wonderful occasion for your child, and he or she will look forward to it every year.

It is not the amount of time, but the quality of time that is important in building meaningful relationships. Keep it easy and interact with your kid in ways that work for you and your family. Connections are long-lasting and give your kid with the assistance they need.

Rules to follow for child when they are outside:

1. No screaming and yelling
2. No throwing , hitting or pushing
3. Teasing or taunting others
4. No lying to anyone
5. Put waste in garbage leave the place as you find it or better
6. Never be alone with strangers
7. Be respectful and polite
8. Never use bad words

# Pay Attention To The State Of His Mind

Dear mommies

Parents are expected to pay attention to two separate areas of their child's growth: the child's physical development and their child's mental development. Some of the senses that are vital during the growth of the child are: hearing, vision, smelling and tasting, ability to speak and feeling pain; these are the fundamental improvements in the child's mental development, and they help the child in the perception of the general occurrences in the world around the child. This is the moment when a parent is able to identify whether or not a kid has a mental or physical issue. When a kid has gained the essential senses to the important aspects of life, which is when they will be able to make persistent images of stuff, even if those objects are not there at the time the image is generated. You are obligated to treat your children with tenderness and love at all times, even if they are outside the home. This includes avoiding assaulting, screaming, yelling, striking, or lying to them. You shouldn't even consider about forgetting it as many mental disorders and difficulties are handed down from one generation to the next. When parents are excessively antagonistic toward their children, it inhibits the kids from maturing in a normal, secure environment. They are capable of becoming angry as well as sensitive at times. They will not forget how they were treated by you, and this will be the key element that leads them to resent you once they are adults. Memories will come pouring back.

If you are worried about a kid, it may be good to encourage them to talk about their fears. Children could become aloof and disturbed when there are troubles at home, such as when their parents are squabbling, when they are divorcing, or when there is a death in the family. They should be encouraged to ask questions if they are puzzled about what has transpired, and they should be reassured that you will do everything in your ability to keep them safe. Avoid taking your kids to mental diseases. Children who have mental health issues are more likely to acquire long-term health problems that will follow them throughout their lives. A child's emotional well-being has no direct effect on their physical well-being. Co-occurring problems affect 40% of all children who have been diagnosed with a mental disease, which means they have more than one mental disorder at once. When a young person already has a mental illness, their chances of developing other mental illnesses as an adult are greatly raised. It is more difficult for adults with mental illness to get a job and contribute productively to their communities because of their condition.

That's why taking into consideration their mental health is very important and it's related to their personality, and the way you treat them is more and more important. So if you want your child to grow and become a normal adult, it's on you to help and accompany him in his trip.

It will definitely work:

1. Allow your child to express their creativity
2. Help your child to solve their problem
3. Create opportunities for your child to express success
4. Help them to be the best they are
5. Be a role model for your child and react positively to them
6. Sometime respect your child's oppositions
7. Don't over pressure child
8. Teach them that how to deal with failure
9. Spend quality time at least once a day
10. Treat them like a adult kids love it

# Children Are The Greatest Gift

I am aware that the pleasure that your youngster enjoys is the most valuable gift that any of you could possibly have.

A young kid is qualified to obtain a broad selection of excellent things. A companion animal is, in my view, the best gift for a young youngster. I have two fundamental reasons for having these thoughts. To begin, owning a pet may be an extremely informative experience. Second, a tiny child may find a pet to be a fantastic friend and comrade. Due to these characteristics, I am of the view that a pet provides for the perfect gift for a young youngster. In addition, a kid could learn about the numerous periods of life by keeping a pet. A young youngster has a lot to acquire by witnessing how their pet evolves over time as pets mature much more swiftly than humans do.

It is beneficial to develop a trustworthy relationship, also known as a stable attachment, with the children in your life by letting them know that you love them for who they are now as well as who they will become in the future. Create a better link with your youngster by engaging in activities that they enjoy and paying attention to the things that they are enthused about during this time together. During these moments, you should resist from being side-tracked by other things, such as activities around the house or electronic devices. It is vital to indicate to your youngster that you are focused on them, despite the fact that it is frequently not only tempting but often necessary to complete more than one task at a time.

When a baby is wounded or furious, it is necessary for them to cry and scream, but as children get older, we don't want them to express their feelings in this way any longer. Children's brains grow at various speeds, and as their language develops, they take on a more active part in selecting how best to convey their feelings. You should let them speak anything they want to say and apologize if they are correct if they are not.

As a parent, you can demonstrate your love and improve your connection with your kid in various ways, including singing with them, playing with them, going outdoors with them, hearing them talk about their difficulties, and going on adventures with them.

Not only can parents influence what their children learn, but also the manner in which their children acquire it. Young people who are unable to accomplish a task may experience frustration, which may lead them to try harder or even quitting up. In order for children to have a good attitude about the process of learning anything new, it is the responsibility of their parents to demonstrate to them that it takes time, effort, commitment, and patience to do so. Finally try to always be someone soft in the way you talk to them to make them feel that they are in a security zone.

Once in a week:

1. Help someone out either it's a friend or someone else
2. Do something special for your parents
3. Do a good deed for mother earth and plantation
4. Read good books and educate yourself
5. Offer Help

## It's ok to be a "messy mom"

Trying to be or to become perfect is a disease that will destroy you over time. We are intrinsic suppliers, we are the fixers. The glue that keeps everything and everyone together. But the moms with the shredded back-story, who wake up every morning to be the greatest versions of themselves, well, those are the mothers I know. I'm not trying to imply that if your life isn't chaotic and confusing then you aren't a good mother. Just to clarify, what I'm trying to say is that the majority of us are wonderful mothers who also happen to be chaotic and complicated. At times, it seems like no one else understands what we are going through. Sometimes, for a variety of reasons, we attempt to cover up that messiness. We don't want people to remember us as the disorganized or disorganized ones; we don't want to be known as such.

It's alright to take a break, if you are exhausted, it's all okay being exhausted. Every mother needs some rest to be strong again, your kids and hubby are here also to understand you. Your health matters too, if you care about everyone else, they should care about your health too. Especially mental health, which it's essential to recognize is always tied to your physical health, and if one of the two is disordered the other will go down too.

It is OK to be aggravated when anything goes wrong in the home since ultimately it is up to you to make things right. Don't be in a hurry to make challenging choices. You simply have to do your best to keep your anxiety under control so that it won't hurt your health or the health of others.

It's OK to admit that it's hard for you and to ask for assistance when you find yourself in need of it; in fact, most people respond positively when you do so. Because he is your partner, your spouse will like it very much as well, and he will want to help you take care of things just as much as you do.

I don't care if your home is a disaster. It is a natural occurrence, and you do not need to keep the home in perfect order at all times. However, everyone in your household should learn how to clean, and they should assist you in doing so. You are not the only one living in the home, nor are you the only one accountable for the upkeep and upkeep of the house.

It is perfectly OK for you to provide sweets as a bribe to your children in the hope that they will act appropriately or do their schoolwork. This is a strategy that many parents use, and it is successful since it produces such positive outcomes. Children are quite receptive to receiving presents, and candy in particular, but you shouldn't provide too many gifts or bribes to them or they may come to see this as the only way to learn the rules or follow instructions.

It's OK that your kids have screen time; in fact, it may be beneficial to their mental health if you monitor what they see on the screen. Set limitations, but don't let them watch too much. Because the children of this generation were born during such an incredible period of technological advancement, they can't live as their parents did. Everyone is on their schedule and has their own life.

It is normal to feed the baby with formula milk for some time. Even doctors will counsel moms on this when the mother is distressed or unable to provide milk so that the mother does not feel nervous while she feeds the baby with formula milk and continues to feed the baby with formula milk.

It is a fantastic thing to take pleasure in the time you spend in the washroom since it is the only time you have to yourself. You should take care of your body and ensure that it receives the restorative benefits that come from getting enough sleep. Your spirit will be rejuvenated, which will provide you with the energy to be powerful, and your intellect will be awoken with new concepts to consider. The finest opportunity to think about a broad variety of subjects is afforded by the period spent unwinding in the washroom, which I refer to as "renewing thoughts." You could find yourself making choices and pursuing paths that you had not previously considered.

Please keep in mind that you are not the only mother who has feelings of disorganization or brokenness. Not even one ounce of it. This is a feeling that the great majority of us have, at some point in our lives, being able to relate to. We all have things; some of them are big, some are little, and others of them we just can't describe; it's OK if you don't know what they are. It is quite OK to be unorganized; in fact, the majority of successful women are. The fact that we are such a disorganized mess is also what gives us our strength and resiliency. We did not get to this point by being fortunate and having things go well for us. Because of the challenges that we have overcome, we are stronger now than we were before. Because we continue to go forward despite the reality that we are complex and a mess. We keep trying.

I am not going to provide an apology for how cluttered my apartment is. Even though not every aspect of who I am is pleasant or easily explained, this is who I am. This constitutes a large portion of all of us. Not only is it commendable to be able to view things in their true light, but it may also be very freeing.

# Part :5

## Why today's parents are under so much pressure?

The job of a parent is a difficult one that requires tenacity, dedication, and most importantly, complete and total devotion. Parenting in the modern world is substantially more difficult than it was in the past as a result of the changing culture and the different perspectives that have emerged about the practices and values of families. It is an understatement to think of the job of parenting as only meeting the child's physiological and psychological needs. Parents, on a day-to-day basis, are greeted with a diverse array of thrilling events, each of which requires an immediate reaction.

The past was a far better time than the present because we lived in a society where neighbours looked out for one another and extended a helping hand to anybody who needed assistance. When you get married, you suddenly find yourself surrounded by a large number of people who love you and are willing to lend a hand in caring for your children. However, after you have children, you discover that everyone is preoccupied with their own lives and that nobody cares about you or your children, not only in a physical sense but also in a mental and financial one. This is what happens when you move away from your family and attempt to start a new life with your spouse and your children on your own. I will tell you that family is more important than anything else in this life, and once they are gone you will realize how much you missed out on they are gone. The assistance that you will need for yourself and your children is very important, and it helps you live a healthy life. Working for money is the most difficult challenge that modern parents face daily, and they don't know where the solution is hiding. However, the assistance that you will need for yourself and your children is very important. Without forgetting the problems that parents can experience in their life like losing their jobs which it's necessary for their living. It's another traumatic thing that parents encounter is job loss. It is uncertain when a job will be lost. In most circumstances, parents who lose their means of sustenance may not have alternative work open to them while still dealing with utility expenditures such as electricity, water, and gasoline, not to mention the basic requirements. There are occasions when parents do not create enough revenue to sustain their family financially.

A huge family is nearly typically a happy family. When parents have a big number of children, they no longer contemplate divorce. Being a parent is always demanding, although our children may encourage us to work harder in both our personal and professional life. I will be joyful, which will contribute to economic success; it will also play an essential role in the mental growth.

Furthermore, when our parents approach retirement age and are unable to work, we may depend on our kids. Growing up, graduating college, and having a career offers delight and pride to their parents. Children will care for their parents when they are in need, and when their parents die, they will inherit the poverty that their parents and forefathers left for them.

The more children we have, however, the more money we need. Because civilization is changing, the standard of living continues to grow. Parents are unable to afford education, food, and child care. It's impossible to provide attention to each member of a huge family, which leads to arguments between the children.

The strength of the bonds that hold the family together is much more important than the size of the family. It is critical to the growth of relationships that both parties prioritize their connections with one another, maintain open lines of communication, and provide mutual support. Interactions within families are what constitute our reality as it is now; they affect both how we perceive things and how we behave in various situations.

People who put high importance on the connections they have with their friends and family tend to have better physical health and report higher levels of happiness. Friendships affect a person's well-being, even though one should not put all of their eggs in one particular basket. This leads to increased comprehension as well as cognitive development as a consequence. Many individuals discover that having supportive connections makes it much simpler for them to deal with stressful situations and advances their development.

When life becomes tough, there will be a greater urge to lean on those who are going through the same thing as you are. When you get together with old acquaintances again, you can find that they have grown up or that they have changed totally.

To increase the likelihood that you will live a long life, you need to maintain positive relationships with everyone in your life, from your family to your friends. This is exactly what the parents of today need to know and comprehend: the fact that their children's lives will become more challenging if they choose to live independently. Even if our time here is limited, we can make the most of what we have by focusing our attention on things like happiness and physical well-being. It's all about our decision and our way of looking at life.

# Part-6

# A message to my children
# " When Life Get Tough"

*" It's important to be yourself and not a fake picture to satisfy other."*

# Self Help And Personal Development.

When I told me, it means my spirit and my power. It's important to be yourself and not a fake picture to satisfy other. Being authentic means accepting yourself just the way you are. Being true to who you are requires you to go through life without concern for what other people think of the way you do it. And all that implies is that you have respect for yourself. It is a complete waste of time to worry about what other people will think since you have no power to influence them or the views that they have. It's very important for your development and the evolution of your personality.

### 1/Self Sufficiency

Every person in this life has his way to live, to see, to love, and a specific road to reach his own dreams. You are amazing by your own imprints, and you don't need to be accompanied to be strong. Your strength is inside your heart you are enough for yourself. Unlike a caged bird, you possess free will and the ability to act according to your own desires, and you have the right to choose what makes you happy. Facing life isn't tough if you know the correct attitude to apply at the appropriate moment. However, there are times when you need to look big to every side in order to realize the truth, and a positive attitude is what will lead you to the light at the end of the tunnel. People may listen to what you have to say and comprehend what you are trying to convey, but they sense your attitude. People will evaluate you based on your attitude, so do not allow the attitudes of others shape your own;

instead, focus on projecting an image that is true to who you are and what you stand for.

**2/ A mistake is always a lesson**

You should not let the fact that you have a lot of experience to lead you to believe that you are incapable of making mistakes. It is pointless to strive for perfection since no one is without flaws in their own lives. In point of fact, one might argue that the pursuit of perfection is a disease, since it leads so many people to run away in terror and end up miserable.

**3/ you live your opinion**

Your own approach to handle difficulties is the best way to live a calm existence; you will use your intellect to work through the issues, and you will make choices that are consistent with the rationale you use. When you are among other people, it is possible that they may affect you, and most people prefer to do the same things that others do and forget who they are and how they think. If you choose to listen to their point of view, then where will you place your own? If you believe that your viewpoint isn't flawless, let me assure you that imperfection is an essential component of flawlessness.

**4/There is no better time**

You are the leader of your own life because if you aren't, life will lead you, and you should never wait for the good moment because you have to make it. Since you are the owner of your time, you will invent the best moment to do what it is that you want to do, and you shouldn't let the opinions of others influence your own. Believing in your yourself is the strongest weapon you can have with no fears to fight every obstacle you may face, surprises will never stop, and it's this is life, and normality isn't what describe it.

### 5/ it's not ego it's self-respect

Through misery, problems, you may be doomed in darkness if you didn't turn on the light, and the light will be always in self-respect, so always dare to love yourself. You will hear some people say that if you want other to respect you, you have to respect them but it's a big mistake. The greatest approach to be appreciated by other people is to first respect and value yourself. You can only get other people to respect you if you respect yourself first. People will only respect you if you do. In other words, you should always be kind to yourself. There is no such thing as a "given gift" that you can hand out to others and expect them to accept or reject you. We must constantly remember that we're dealing with a person and not a thing. The secret to a happy life is learning to love and accept oneself. When you love everything about yourself, without conditions, life will mirror that love back to you in some way. Learning to love oneself completely is the first step in cultivating a joyful and supportive environment in which to thrive. When we lose sight of what is most essential to us–loving ourselves–we also lose sight of our goals and aspirations, as well as being happy and healthy in our lives. In the end, to live a life that is meaningful demands, first and foremost, that you love all aspects of who you are and have faith that the world loves you in the same way.

### 6/ Ask for help you are not weak

If you choose yourself, you may find yourself stronger, independent with your own way and specific power, but sometimes life will be very difficult without any compassion or pity. It will harm you and hurt your spirit, and try to turn off your light and here the existence of help that you must never be shy to ask, because life is supposed to be like that. You don't have to feel bad about asking for assistance. Everyone, regardless of age or stage of life, needs help at some point in time. Good and strong people know very well the importance of help to struggle darkness. An arrogant person's lack of faith in the purity of others is a form of excessive pathological self-love that makes it difficult to love, and it's sometimes referred to as Pathological narcissism. Helping others was always the opposite of arrogant people, who will fail in life because they lack faith in the purity of others. This is why it's necessary to maintain a state of normalcy in your thoughts and actions, so that others can see how white your heart is and come to you for aid.

**7/ Giving never made anybody poor**

When they ask for aid, you'll gladly lend a hand to make them happy and enjoy the satisfaction of knowing that you've made their lives better. You don't want to end yourself in a negative scenario by becoming involved in the other person's dilemma. Some people will not give you access to their life, accordingly, walk with the rule that says help when you hear them ask.

In the end personal development is a never-ending process. Assessing one's strengths and limitations, as well as one's hopes and objectives in life, is a vital step towards fulfilling one's maximum potential.

# Personal And Social Life

We are living in a world that will never fiRosie, we may die and another generation will come to replace us. A normal person in the society is someone who knows how to manage his work and his personal life. Your good work will make you a successful person but you don't have to put yourself through hell in order to achieve success. Working hard isn't what gets you ahead; working intelligently is what gets you there, and a smart person will always be aware of the path that is best for him to pursue for his own welfare. Creating a schedule that works for you is a commitment to yourself that you will fiRosie your most critical responsibilities. Planning your day in advance might help you avoid get bogged down in the details of the daily grind.

**1/ achieving a balance between work and personal life**

You must work hard to become a successful person, but never forget that your objective is to live a happy life with your family. You can't be successful in business if your personal life is a mess. You'll err Identify the skills, information, resources, or tools that will prevent repetition, yet it's always acceptable to make errors. You'll learn to refuse everyone who attempts to be a barrier and say no in front of everyone. It's alright to be selfish and love yourself is a sacred priority. When you're angry, upset, or depressed, don't be afraid to weep to release the bad energy from your heart.

**2/ really be there for your partner**

A nice life between you and your spouse demands a lot of knowledge to make persist forever full with love and honesty. The spouse you will live with is a unique individual from your own ideas; don't expect to locate a clone of yourself. That distinctiveness makes life lovely. You have to be independent and not a slave for his dictates. Discussing is the finest strategy remedy troubles be sure you will have to face them and a lot of issues are waiting for you, but you have to be wise and you have to learn how to compromise and achieve a solution which will please you both, and provide your love, and trust, because with it you will win his heart and soul. We hear about some couple who were divorced over a tiny problem, but what we didn't notice is that the lack of reasonable and fair expectation is what leads to divorce regularly. Divide your household to make sure that no one is obliged to work for the other. Everyone inside the household had the same value and for being financially independent is something basic.

**3/ house rules to obey**

The house must be an organized place because it's the source of great people. We hear the greatest persons were born in such a discipline place. For that you have to be a great person inside the house exactly like outside, and there will be no harm. Refrain from touching or stepping on anyone's hands or feet. No interruptions. Wait until it's your time to talk before you begin. There is no shouting allowed in the home. Speaking in the home requires the employment of an internalized tone of voice. Furniture should not be climbed or jumped on. On the sofa or on the bed, relax. You are going to switch on something, remember that a decent person will realize that shutting off it is your job. It's true that love is full in the home but it doesn't imply if you borrow anything you don't have to return it as quickly as possible, it includes also remove it from its spot. Your brothers or sister or even your parents will not know how you think, and of course if it isn't yours the approval you will obtain is an obligation. Sometimes you will have troubles in the home and when you didn't control yourself and said something unpleasant, apologize without any hesitation to make your connection full with respect to the others and full with compassion and love.

**4/pay attention of family problems**

In every family there are much of problems, but only the great and the intelligent one survive and wouldn't divide because of it. There are conflicting personalities and debates on the best method to accomplish a task. Brothers and sisters quarrel or jealously. Assume taking care is a method to demonstrate how grownup you are. Try to be discreet in your family life by keeping things from other family member so you will not generate issues of jealously and keep your secrets to yourself, which isn't required doesn't need to be known. Do never defend bad decisions but only the correct one, and preserve always your positive attitude for not participating into a poisonous behavior, or unneeded drama that aggravates any issue in the family. Our families absorb many of the tensions and stresses from the outside world and the pressures may boil over. Sometimes a personal problem, particularly in a young kid, may overwhelm a family and there seems to be no visible road forward. At other times changes inside the family leave other members bewildered and angry or sad. A toxic member of your family should be cut off from your life as soon as possible, since he or she will have a long-term negative impact on your well-being. You don't have to endure falsehoods or disrespect or drama; remember that your life is a holy, magnificent gift. Even if no one has informed them, children and teens frequently blame themselves for family difficulties. Changes in the family might make youngsters uncomfortable and self-conscious. They're furious, nervous, or sad. This affects school and friendships. That's why it's important to avoid family politics.

**5/ helping means white-hearted**

Charity is providing love, thus don't merely contribute money, but stretch out your hand instead. Always attempt to assist everyone whether financially or emotionally. It will make you feel better and not just them. With support you will show the others how human you are, and your relief will continue from generation to generation. You will be renowned with such a fantastic name. It's usually recorded in novels and tales how decent individuals serve the others without taking any advantage. People perform nice things and serve others simply for tranquility and only for having a pleasant life. When you offer people a nice life, be sure you will have one greater than theirs because our god will protect you constantly and will provide you gifts to assure you. Even if you believe it's without benefit but the fact is you are experiencing serenity from within to outside. Try to comprehend the other maybe he will need simply a kind word a touch from you so he will retain his strength again. Spread your excellent energy to everyone and never be hesitant to provide your positive force to everyone.

# Always Prioritize Your Health

Right now, it's vital that we all concentrate on taking care of our health. People sometimes disregard their normal health problems owing to their demanding schedules and other duties. Always follow your doctor's directions if you have a long-term medical concern. Even if we typically feel good, we may all benefit from checking in on how we are doing in areas that influence our well-being. If we do not take appropriate measures to maintain our health, we will notice that it has changed. When it comes to living a normal, disease-free life, having a healthy mental and social well-being is just as important as having a good physical well-being. To maintain your physical well-being, you need to give careful consideration to every facet of your life, beginning from the inside and working your way out. Life's balance is always about how will you choose to live, the manner you pick is the reality of your health; take it into account very carefully.

**1/ Physical health:**

If you walk at least 5,000 steps every day, you will lower your risk of developing several different illnesses. You will manage or prevent a variety of illnesses, such as diabetes type 2, cancer, high blood pressure, stroke, and heart disease. Improve cardiovascular fitness. Train your muscles and bones to become stronger. Improve muscular endurance. Raise your overall level of energy. Low blood pressure, reduced heart disease and stroke risk, avoidance of some malignancies, lower risk of eye and digestive issues, and a good impact on blood sugar may all be ascribed to a diet heavy in vegetables and fruits, which may also help regulate appetite, and without forgetting drinking water which is very important for your health with a quantity about 10 cups. You put yourself at danger of being dehydrated if you don't consume enough water on a daily basis. Weakness, low blood pressure, dizziness, disorientation, and dark-coloured urine are all warning indications of dehydration. Other symptoms include dry mouth and skin. go screen-free at mealtimes I don't have a blanket aversion to screens, but I do think they prevent children from developing skill sets that are necessary in specific situations. Practice mindful eating, many of us start by listening to our ideas, but we may obtain more insight by first listening to our body. Instead of eating when we're anxious, upset, disappointed, lonely, or bored, we may listen to our body. Another method to get a physical health is meditation which helps in gaining a new perspective on stressful situations, building skills to manage your stress, increasing self-awareness, focusing on the present, and reducing negative emotions. Also another useful method, meditation helps develop a fresh perspective on difficult events, strengthen stress-management skills, increase self-awareness, concentrate on the present, and reduce negative emotions. In the end don't forget to use fasting every week it helps you to eliminate toxicity from your body and also weekly meal pre planning.

**2/ screen free meal:**

It may be good for you to know precisely how you are spending your time while you are using your phone, thus it is recommended that you refrain from using social media over the weekend or for at least one day. You want to put yourself in the best position to succeed, so choose a favourable weekend. If you are going to give up anything, you should make sure that the item you are giving up is something that you really believe is worthwhile. Alternately, the time that you would have spent on social media should be spent doing something else. You should read at least one page of an excellent book every day to keep your mental health in check. Reading is good for your mental health, a Form of Entertainment That Does Not Cost Anything, increases one's ability to concentrate as well as their ability to focus, improves one's ability to read and write, helps one have better sleep, it improves one's general knowledge, a Great Way to Get Motivated, and it helps to lower stress levels. Always feel with gratitude because it's a potent trigger for happiness, In addition, if you ever find yourself stressed out by anything or someone, write it down and don't forget to practice the spiritual mantra. If you do what I've instructed, your soul will be at ease. Also, love must always be expressed verbally; never keep it bottled up within yourself. If you care about someone, tell him. However, even if the individual refuses to tell you the truth, you will feel better knowing it. Create your own serenity if you feel the world is too noisy, and you'll discover that the balance in your life will be easier to maintain. There is a question that you have to pose to yourself, what is my biggest weakness? When you identify the solution, the following step is to clip it off. Don't be cocky and don't underestimate yourself, and share an example of how you've tried to build upon your deficiency or develop a new ability to battle the problem. A lazy day is a good opportunity to take off from work and enjoy some leisure time without feeling guilty about it, but not always relaxation will take you down. Successful individuals detest sleeping. Your health will emerge on your eyes and attitude. Your physical health and mental health are related don't ever separate your physic from your mental and for that avoid bad habits and junk food, it's not only a waste for your money and time but a destruction which will eat you by time and make you hooked for bad habits.

**3/Social health**

Everything in this world is interrelated, including your physiological and mental well-being, and this is no exception. Turn off your phone, spend time with your loved ones, cook a meal together, go for a stroll after dinner, select a book to read with them, and schedule a day vacation every month. Put together a group of people who will encourage you and provide you with new points of view by being part of a network of people who have your back. Negative and toxic people who are always seeking for methods to injure others or talk about themselves should not be a part of your life. You should avoid associating with such people. When having a conversation on a topic, you should never bring up the personal lives of other people. Try to keep your expectations in check and center your energy on finding peace among a close-knit community of people who really care about you and value what you bring to the table. Never be a negative person; instead, make it your mission to lead a happy, enthusiastic life. It is essential that you show your partner proper respect at all times and work to ensure that he or she is content whenever you are in their company. It is vitally important to have close relationships with other people in order to live a longer and better life, therefore avoid isolating yourself from the rest of the world. In addition to alleviating pain, it encourages healthy habits and either delays the start of memory loss or Alzheimer's disease altogether or prevents it entirely.

# Failing Is Not Deadly.

Asking oneself, "What does success and failure genuinely mean?" is a worthwhile exercise. People's views on success and failure are often the subject of impassioned debate because of their wide range of viewpoints. These two difficulties confront everyone at some point in their lives. There isn't a correct response. The two definitions are almost always mutually inclusive. Success and failure may be defined in a variety of ways. For example, if you don't fail, it's considered a victory. As a result, I feel that success and failure are intertwined and can only be judged by how hard one tries to learn from their mistakes.

Failure is inevitable for everybody who believes they are capable of accomplishing their goals. As a result, people may have two contrasting views of themselves: either they are a failure or they are successful. However, I'm not convinced. It's possible that there's a middle ground. If you want to succeed, you first have to fail. You may learn from someone who has achieved success. How, for instance, will you continue to be successful? Is it possible to be successful even if you fail at one step? To succeed, one must first comprehend the consequences of failure.

It's human nature to steer clear of anything that has even a remote chance of failing. It may be really embarrassing and unpleasant to feel when you fail at anything. It's not good to be hard on yourself about mistakes you've made in the past. In the long run, it will just make you feel worse than you already do. As a consequence of this, you will reply with a negative answer given that failing is only one of the necessary steps to follow.

In order to be successful, the first thing a person has to do is give up trying to fail. The psychological effect of being successful is far larger than that of just completing a goal. It is possible to have feelings of achievement even when one is confronted with challenging circumstances. To have a sense of fulfillment, it is essential to have some level of success. How frequently do you let yourself feel like you've triumphed over something?

It is important to not be afraid of failure because even when things go wrong, you may learn a lot from them. It is possible that in the long term, it will serve as a very valuable lesson for us. It is my hope that we will be able to comprehend it and get wisdom from it. Conducting a failure analysis and identifying the underlying causes of a failure is one of the most productive methods to gain knowledge from past mistakes. When our job or the firm we work for is successful, it's reassuring to know that. On the other side, feedback based on our failures gives us the chance to improve ourselves by studying what we did wrong. Failures that occur early on in a project are sometimes referred to as experiments because of their nature. These failures might serve as a springboard for innovative ideas that eventually lead to higher levels of success.

The hopes and objectives that people have for their lives may be seen reflected in their dreams. They are the engine that has propelled mankind to its highest heights of success. Dreams have the ability to motivate people to set long-term objectives and desires for themselves. At some time in their life, each and every person has entertained the idea of doing anything. The pursuit of one's desires is the primary motivation for all of one's acts and attitudes. In order to accomplish what you set out to do, you have to keep working toward your objectives and putting in the time and effort required to do so.

One definition of creativity is "the potential to develop something new that did not exist before." Having a creative mind and using your imagination gives you a distinct advantage, allowing you to do amazing things. You may be able to triumph over difficulties in this life by engaging in creative thought. When it comes to leading a pleasant and financially successful life, creativity is a natural prerequisite for success in life. The ability to use one's imagination is essential for the development of new ideas, a requirement for many different types of careers, and is of the utmost significance for the healthy development of children. Having a vivid imagination is really necessary in order to build a successful career. Sometimes, the success of your profession depends on how inventive you are.

You must be consistent in your work, and to be consistent, you must accomplish the same good things over and over again until they become your identity. Humans are hardwired to be inconsistent. It's exhausting at first, but it gets easier after a time. It requires a lot of energy, which is becoming increasingly restricted. Attempting to accomplish too much at once will merely make the task more difficult. You won't be able to create a new, healthy habit in a handful of days. Always take things one step at a time as our minds aren't trained to think that way. The brain demands a lot of energy. As a consequence, we may feel intellectually sluggish or tired when presented with a task, such as consistency. Don't be tricked. Take the lead. Try to disregard your feelings. Because if you don't, you will remain entangled, and be always strong

The value of putting forth effort and working hard is something that can never be overstated. It is quite difficult to achieve excellence without putting in a lot of effort. To put it another way, a person who chooses to sit and wait for something else in lieu of engaging in productive activity cannot get anything. About the other side, a person who keeps working hard consistently will certainly gain success in life, and this is exactly what will be covered in the essay that is going to be written on hard labour.

## Time To Re-Evaluate Your Circle.

You may either rise or fall in your friendships and interactions with other individuals. There is no need in clinging to a toxic relationship that has been out of the picture for years because we still have some emotional connection from our side but if it is not mutual between two persons, then there is no point in keeping it around. This is why it's so vital that we pick the proper form of relationship or friendship for ourselves.

If you are serious about advancing ahead in life or your work, you should interact with folks who are already at the top of their field. It is possible to extend your thinking and open yourself up to new ideas in this manner. It's OK to feel at comfortable around others who share your interests.

If you want to become the person you want to be now and in the future, you need to venture out of your comfort zone and spend time with individuals who can expose you to new experiences and bring you fresh information about the higher level of life. In order to get ahead in life, you need take advantage of these friendships.

Make friends with folks who share your main ideas. Diversity is a fantastic thing in many aspects, but when it comes to our basic values and views, it's best to stick to friendships with those who share those values and beliefs.

The value of having a companion with whom you share similar objectives cannot be emphasized. Because you share a similar purpose, you may create a partnership to start a new firm, and you can both push and encourage one other, which will improve your friendship.

Negative people are more likely to intimidate and dissuade you, thus it's better to surround yourself with positive people. Negative people should be kept at least a mile away from everyone, since they have more power than positive people. Having an immediate effect on you is possible. Sayings like "This is not something that you could achieve" or "I don't believe you can do this" serve as good examples. You shouldn't be friend with someone who has such hazardous views; it's not good for either of you. Don't get too close to those who are hooked to substances like alcohol and drugs as well as those who believe that money is the root of all evil.

If you want to be a better person, you need to surround yourself with individuals who are willing to learn. It's all about learning, and the more we learn, the better we become. So being in the company of someone who is eager to learn new things will have a good effect on you and push you to do the same. It's important to be aware that the people and places you choose to surround yourself with will shape who you become.

Your future will be shaped by the people you spend the most time with, so be sure you choose them wisely.

## Parents Are The Biggest Of All The Blessing In This World

Keep in mind that your parents were always there for you, with your mother leaving her work and your father putting up a battle every day just for you.

As our parents age, their requirements could shift to accommodate their changing needs. On the other side, you may be at a loss as to how to provide a helping hand or even where to begin doing so.

Children are often the members of a person's family who are able to jump in and provide the most immediate assistance to an old person if the person has relatives, which suggests that you are one of those children.

When caring for your parents, there are a number of things you need to keep in mind, including the support of your family, the safety of your house, the medical needs of your parents, the cognitive health of your parents, mobility, personal hygiene, food preparation, and social interaction.

When a person is already concerned about losing their independence, the last thing they want to do is give up any further control over their lives. As a consequence of this, it is of the utmost importance that you include your parent in the process of preparing for their care as much as is reasonably feasible. Because of this, rather of seeing you as an outsider who has swooped in to make a difference, people will see you as a collaborator who is working with them. It is likely that you will need to have more than one conversation with them in order to get through to them. Do not force someone to make changes too quickly unless there is an immediate threat to their safety. Beginning with baby steps and working your way up to larger amounts of support is the best way to approach this. Make sure that the floors and walkways are clear of any carpets, wires, and other debris that may be there. A grab bar system is also being placed in each of the bathrooms, in addition to a stair railing system that is being put throughout the whole home. Performing maintenance on the lights to ensure that it is bright in all areas and that the switches can be reached without difficulty. Doing checks on all of the machinery and verifying that everything is operating correctly. Eliminating the need for using a step stool or a stooping position

Keep a tight eye on their well-being; you are ultimately accountable for it. Late-life health difficulties are fairly commonplace. Many older adults have long-term medical conditions that require constant medication and monitoring. A family member's support may be necessary if an aged person gets new symptoms or has new health conditions that need medical treatment. In many situations, family members are the ones who go to the physicians with questions and concerns. The majority of persons will also require support in the case of a health catastrophe. Elderly persons may become incapable of making their own health care decisions or managing their own care as a consequence of major disease or certain chronic conditions. Because of a medical emergency or mental decline, family members are frequently pushed to make judgments.

## Be A Smart Money Manager

You must keep an eye on your financial status if you want to prepare for the future. Investing your money correctly is just as crucial as earning money. Recognize and track the flow of your money resources. Managing your money may be simpler if you raised your savings. You don't simply gain from saving money when you're in a terrible condition. When the perfect occasion presents itself, you may take advantage of your savings and double, triple, or even quadruple your money. Preparing for the future involves preserving money. For a better future, money management programs propose that you enhance both your wages and your savings. The practice of managing one's money does not halt each month and begin again the following month.

Because money is such a vital element of your life, you should approach it with considerable prudence. The quality of a person's life is determined by the quantity of money he or she has to spend. It controls where you can live, how excellent your health care is, how good your education is, and everything else you need to have a happy life.

Put some thinking into whether or not what you're attempting to purchase is worth your money. Try to live your life in a way that is as simple as possible. If you don't need it, don't take on too many duties. You have to let go of things from time to time if you want to preserve your balance. When it comes to money management and personal finance, the two are connected. Depending on how skillfully you utilize them, you may be enjoying a life of financial stability or suffering. It all boils down to what you learn as an adolescent. When it comes to money management, you don't have to put yourself in a bind all the time. Friends and family members who are struggling financially could benefit from many of the lessons learnt. As a consequence, it's crucial that you stay knowledgeable of the ideal strategies for managing your cash.

Another thing to keep in mind is that your spouse will be with you for the rest of your life, so it's crucial to select carefully. By selecting a girl who simply loves money, you'll lose everything and never advance in life. One of the most problematic concerns for couples is money. The most vital words to bear in mind when it comes to marriage and money, no matter how unpleasant they may be, are: Always speak the truth. Honesty is as crucial in a relationship as it is in any financial conversation. Divorce procedures may be launched if a spouse is misled to about their financial condition. Don't be persuaded by the temptation. In order to keep on top of house costs, you'll need to speak about your long-term savings and retirement goals. As a consequence of this, selecting the appropriate partner is of the utmost importance.

Believe me when I say that if you want to live a beautiful life that is full of pleasure and tranquillity, you need to make sure that you are a competent money manager.

# Part -6

# Letter To My Children.

First and foremost, I want to convey my everlasting love for you. I wish you realized how much it affects me when you talk about individuals who damage your feelings. I mask my sorrow to display my strength while supporting you in understanding, managing, and dealing with those youngsters. I wish you realized how proud I am of you. For a guy, the world is different , you have to be strong, take care of your wife and children, and become a wise man who know justice and learn how to be a good man for you partner, and you have to realize that not everything in this life comes with force, sometimes you have to use your mind, also for a female the world is totally different, you have to be strong, independent woman, don't forget that after marriage you have another responsibility is taking care of your kids, they are the next generation and a huge percentage of becoming successful depending on you and the way you will take care and educating them, life will show you ups and down just keep the momentum up and never lose hope, the day you will lose it , everything will be vaRosieed, and you are not the same. Each of you has distinct commitments and limits to conform to, and even God has acknowledged that you are unique. That is why you must be bold and fill your heart with faith, love, and tranquility. Life will be tough for you both at times, so stick close to each other during the darkest situations. Your sister is your soul, while your brother is your arm. Learn that love is always there and light is always close by; all you have to do is flip it on.

# A Beautiful Letter To My Daughter For A Better Future

My Dearest Little Love

I'm in awe of how quickly you're maturing, yet I'm also filled with love, grief, and dread. It amazes me how gorgeous and caring you are becoming as a young person. You can instantly brighten the atmosphere of a room with a grin and a burst of enthusiasm. But I'm also terrified of what the world will do to you as you continue your adventure outside of my protecting arms... Sweetheart, you've got a lot going for you. However, this world is difficult and might be filled with dark and frightening things. Keep in mind that compassion is contagious; spread it like wildfire. I want you to fall in love and fall hard, I want you to love sincerely and let yourself be loved. The ability to make difficult decisions and confront difficult situations in life comes from putting your faith in God and following your gut instincts. Fight for what you believe in and don't be scared to speak up for what is right. Regardless of how you feel about yourself, you deserve of everything that life has to offer.

There are times when the world fails to live up to its potential as a wondrous place. There may be times when you are confronted with circumstances that call for understanding and patience on your part. I have a dream that when you are older, you will be a woman who is secure in her own uniqueness and who does not conform to the standards that society sets for what constitutes physical attractiveness. Now that I have spent some time in this world, I have realized, and

I am gradually starting to understand, that my own beauty does not rely on the requirements of fitting into this world, but rather on the intentions that are held inside my heart. I have faith that as my conviction in this proposition deepens, I will also deepen my understanding of how best to communicate this to you.

My darling daughter

1. Appreciate everything and take no one for granted
2. You are the most beautiful than you will ever know
3. Don't let mistake defines you lets from them
4. If someone make you sad and cry more than 4 times, kick them out
5. Maintain your digital privacy
6. Use your voice whenever needed
7. Nourish and take care of your body and mind
8. Don't waste your too much time on worrying
9. If you learn something teach others too
10. Your opinions are important to me
11. You are such a special part of our family

    At last , I love watching you grow into a precious person you were made to be.

# Sweet Letter To My Handsome Son For His Better Future

My dear sweet boy

I am very grateful to have you in my life, and I adore seeing how you develop! I am very pleased of the young man I see you becoming now that you are just starting to exhibit your great personality. As soon as I learned we were expecting a boy, I knew I had chosen the one.

Sweetheart, I wish I could undo some of the traumatic events that have occurred in your early life. I long for a world free of senseless tragedies involving children. The past cannot be changed, and I can't shield you from all the horrible things I wish I could, no matter how hard I try. I can only do my best to educate and lead you, my son. I'd like to believe that by the time you're old enough to discern between good and bad words, I've given you the tools you'll need to do just that. Words that might stick with you for the rest of your life, and I want you to hold on to a few core principles as you develop. Even in the face of adversity, keep spreading compassion. When things are tough, I want you to keep in mind that you should always be strong and courageous. Be courteous, and I expect you to show respect for girls and women as you go in your life. When you treat people with respect, you'll always be the winner. Remember how fortunate you are and hold on to your blessings when you face adversity. Put your family first, but only if the choices you make about your work are actually in the best interest of your loved ones. Simply because that's all you've got at the end of it all, it is always the right choice to do the right thing.

To, my Handsome Son

1. You are a masterpiece
2. You are a gift, our life would not be complete without you
3. Be a protector of those weaker than you
4. Stand up for what's right
5. Be yourself there's no one in the world like you
6. Don't suffer alone ask for help when you need it.
7. Smile and laugh even if its hard
8. Greet people with a smile
9. Pray everyday God is always and forever with you .

# Message To The World

The world has been altered a lot, but together with love and peace we can make it a better place.

Please avoid from pronouncing judgment on other living creatures; every soul in this cosmos is unique.

Don't be a harsh, severe, rough person; instead, be kind and let your words soften at all times, and encourage humanity around the world to make it a better place.

When someone begs for your assistance, do all you can to help them, and make sure you will do that without any advanced benefits, this is the quality people look for inside others. It's the faith in god and love of spirits that will give a shining face full with good acts on you.

Keep a positive attitude of mind; you are what you think.

To have self-respect, one must first love oneself and then behave oneself with respect and decency. Having a feeling of self-respect is crucial, but don't forget to demonstrate respect for others as well.

If you want to move on, you must learn to forgive each other, and if you don't, you'll lose everything. Although no one is infallible, it's necessary to take prudence in the future.

Plantation ideals may be represented by the usage of greenery.

Mother Earth has protected us for a long time, and it's time for us to offer her the respect it deserves.

One day a week, break away from the digital world for at least an hour or two and immerse yourself in nature, enabling your soul to be filled with faith and tranquility.

Let the world a pure, white, peaceful place, don't make dark with wars, diseases and pollution. If death will spread everywhere, we will be doomed in darkness forever. No matter your color, religion, or sexual orientation, you have the right to love whomever you want, and that is my message to the rest of the world.

## Complimentary Tips For Every Mom To Teach Their Child:

1/When you see someone in need please help them

2/Don't be a people's delight that someone should not take advantage of you

3/If you observe a blind person crossing the street, assist them without dismissing them.

4/If someone is starving, please feed them.

5/No body shaming, such as obese or thin, unless you know someone with a health problem.

6/No mockery of others. It's a bad habit, and it makes you a bad person in the eyes of others?

7/No disagreements if you don't agree just leave quietly.

8/ Be intelligent when you talk with other, don't talk only for talking.

9/Remind Them How Much You Believe in Them

10/Respect and Validate Feelings

11/Develop Self-Awareness

12/Share Your Stories with them so they will have your experience and learn from you.

13/Boosting Your Child's Self-Esteem

14/Catch Children Doing Good

15Set boundaries and stick to your discipline.

16/Set aside time for your children.

17/Be an excellent role model.

18/Make it a priority to communicate.

19/Be willing to change your parenting style if necessary.

20/Demonstrate your unconditional love.

21/As a parent, be aware of your own needs and limitations.

22/Face it: Face yourself. You are a flawed parent. As a family leader, you have both strengths and shortcomings. Recognize your strengths. "I am devoted and loving."" Make a promise to work on your flaws. "I need to be more disciplined in my approach."" Try to set reasonable goals for yourself, your spouse, and your children. Be forgiving of oneself without having all the solutions.

Also, make parenting a doable task. Rather of attempting to cover everything at once, concentrate on the areas that need the most attention. When you're exhausted, admit it. Take a break from parenting to do activities that will make you happy as an individual (or as a couple).

It is not selfish to prioritize your needs. It simply shows that you are concerned about your personal well-being, another crucial trait to instil in your children.

# Acknowledgment

Writing a book is harder than I thought and more rewarding than I could have ever imagined. None of this would have been possible without my love man, so I have to start by thanking my awesome husband. From reading early drafts to giving me advice on the cover, he was as important to this book getting done as I was. Thank you so much, dear. My Florentine kids Hridaam and Vani who gave me strength to fiRosie the book and make my world shining with light and ideas. Thank you, God, for the finest gift you've ever given me, another day to live, another chance to have. I'm eternally grateful to any reader of my book.

# Know More About The Author

An author was by profession an instructor I was from very simple background by my constancy and my hard work is the consequence of what I am now. Thank you for delivering your amazing feedback to my previous book "My success wing" as would anticipate similar for this book too. I always enjoy do anything creative and time demandable stuff.

But always eager to try something new, writing a book is my love and even it was my greatest goal to be a writer. My major pastime is reading books and desire other also to spend some quality time in reading., I love to interact with productive peoples enjoy to spend time with nature. I never follow any wealth or poverty. My life basic principles is believe in mankind, live simple lifestyle which cost minimal maintenance, Respect for everybody.

Thank you very much for providing me one more opportunity to express my opinions with you shall look forward for many more. Thanks a lot once again

**Grateful for :**

- Very well-articulated!!! The author has done a fabulous job in getting her thoughts on the paper. Really looking forward to having another book.

  (Monika Taneja)

- She is a supermom with lots of skills. She is very passionate about her work and has a very nice understanding on parenting, child development and social skills.

  (Divya Bandi)

- Her writing style screams she is a person that is innovative and relatable and knows what she writes about. Thanks to the good people of good reads, to Amazing Author.

  (Disha Saxena)

Reviews are the best way to tell an Author thank you and show that you enjoyed their book.

Looking forward for more positive things and your support.

# Thank you